SOCCER

By Mark Littleton

ZondervanPublishingHouse
Grand Rapids, Michigan

A Division of HarperCollinsPublishers

Soccer
Copyright © 1996 by Mark Littleton

Requests for information should be addressed to:

♨ ZondervanPublishingHouse
Grand Rapids, Michigan 49530

Library of Congress Cataloging-in-Publication Data

Littleton, Mark R., 1950–
   Soccer / Mark Littleton.
      p. cm.
   Summary: Several soccer players, including Paul Zimmerman, Desmond
Armstrong, and Jon Payne give testimony to the power of faith in their lives.
   ISBN: 0-310-20264-7
   1. Soccer players—United States—Biography—Juvenile literature.
2. Soccer players—Religious life—United States—Juvenile literature.
[1. Soccer players. 2. Christian life.]   I. Title.   II. Series: Littleton,
Mark R., 1950–   Sports heroes.
GV942.7.A1L58   1996
796.334'092'2—dc 20   96-2350
[B]   CIP
                                    AC

Edited by Tom Raabe
Interior design by Joe Vriend

Printed in the United States of America

96 97 98 99 00 01 02 /❖DH/ 10 9 8 7 6 5 4 3 2

*For Joni and Kelly Littleton,
two nieces with a lot of verve.*

Contents

Soccer's On the Move!

Soccer is a new wrinkle for me as a writer. I've never played soccer except in pickup games in high school. I've never been familiar with the rules, nor have I been much of a fan.

But as I got to know the seven men profiled in this book, how they think, and their experiences as people committed to Christ and to soccer, I found myself inspired. There may be something to this game yet.

I don't think I'm a lot different from the average American. We've all grown up on baseball, football, basketball, and hockey, and have had little time for other sports like soccer. Yet, soccer is one of the more popular sports in the United States for kids. Teams have sprouted up all over the place.

Undoubtedly, soccer is of deep and abiding interest to you or you wouldn't have picked up this book. I hope you'll read these stories with a real sense of joy in your chosen sport. Big things are happening on the soccer scene. Desmond Armstrong tells me that Major League Soccer is right around the corner. And all the fellows profiled in this book tell me there's a lot more to this sport than running around in half circles and kicking.

So I'm watching the news, reading the headlines, and looking for some of the names of those who excel in a sport that is just getting its toehold in

America. Maybe you'll even see the name of one of the guys in this book in lights in the days ahead.

Who knows—maybe you'll even meet one in person as they minister for Jesus and for soccer!

Chapter 1

☆ Brian Davidson ☆

Height: 5 feet, 9 inches

Weight: 180 pounds

Position: Coach

Birth date: March 9, 1960

Team: **Charlotte Eagles** (founder)

Brian Davidson: Opening Doors for the Lord

I always wanted to do something that would impress my dad," Brian Davidson says. "My older brothers were all great in sports. One of them scored 64 points in a high school basketball game. So I grew up with this feeling that I wanted to do well in sports. It happened in my sophomore year in college."

What happened? We'll look at that in a moment. But first, who is Brian Davidson?

Right now he is coach of the Charlotte Eagles, a pro soccer team that travels the world playing the best teams in other countries.

He played many sports as a kid—baseball, basketball, bowling—and at one time thought he'd like to be a professional bowler. However, after he enrolled at Houghton College, he joined a soccer team called Sports Ambassadors, a division of Overseas Crusades, a missions organization. While playing on that team Brian discovered the power of sports to open doors.

"I was at the beginning of a journey which helped me learn to be a sports minister," he says.

Brian discovered soccer's particular appeal. "It's probably the greatest visa in the world," he says, "in particular to the Muslim world. You can take a soccer ball anywhere in this world and have a great chance to spread the gospel. It's amazing. I see how the Lord whittled away all the different sports and focused in on soccer in my life. I enjoyed baseball and basketball and bowling, but the Lord directed me to soccer."

That commitment has ultimately led Brian into twenty-one different countries to play soccer and preach the gospel.

One year the Sports Ambassadors played about a dozen games in India, and won more than they lost.

"To win the respect of foreigners, you have to win," Brian says. "Otherwise, they won't be interested."

Brian and his teammates never played a game in front of less than ten thousand people. In fact, they were mobbed. "We were like Hollywood celebrities," Brian says. "Overseas, soccer is *the* sport! We weren't high on the talent pool compared to these other countries. In fact, it was like Norway putting together a basketball team and coming over to play the NBA. Still, we won more than we lost."

At the games the team gave testimonies at half-time and passed out brochures and literature. After that, they talked with people and invited them to the local church they were connected with. "Again, it was amazing," Brian says. "People would be standing outside to wait and hear us. They'd never go to church on their own. But because it was soccer, they came. That soccer ball opens up doors."

During that first year with Sports Ambassadors Brian gave his testimony at halftime of the second game. As he spoke, he suddenly realized something: he could play soccer in order to make the gospel the priority.

"Sports can be so full of pride, jealousy, anger, envy, self-righteousness. It can be so egotistical. I really felt a call to use the fruit of the Spirit in my life as an athlete.

"It was far more fulfilling than playing soccer just to win games," he says. "Going over there to share my testimony, give out Bibles, and so on gave me a vision for sports ministry. I saw then that soccer could be used by the Lord to spread the news of the gospel. That excited me."

How did Brian become a Christian?

His father was fifty-two and his mom was forty-six when he was born. They already had three sons and a daughter who were over twenty years old. Brian was the surprise.

"My mom had come to know the Lord two years before my birth," Brian says. "She died of cancer on July 4, 1966, when I was six years old. The important thing about her was her prayer life. She prayed with me every day."

That habit of prayer took root in Brian, even though he was still very young. He recalls a time during his mom's illness. "I was still in kindergarten. I was by her bedside and then I ran out the front door to play. But suddenly I remembered the prayer mom and I always had. I ran back in and prayed with her. She was very intent in prayers for me."

Brian's dad tried to raise Brian after his wife died, but he was transferred to another job down south. He had a rough time at his age—sixty—raising an eight-year-old kid. So Brian went to live in Rochester, New York, with his brother, a Presbyterian minister, and his wife.

During those early years, Brian lived for sports. He got off track with the Lord and put Him in a back pocket. He attended church with his brother's family, but complained a lot that people in church were hypocrites and boring. But one day Brian heard a missionary woman speak about her ministry. It fascinated him that this missionary was committed to the Lord the way he was to sports.

Over the years, two missionaries deeply affected him. One was Elsa Logan, who worked in China, and the other was Rose Pinneo, who ministered in Nigeria. "They both really impacted my life," Brian says. "I saw that full commitment. They were both sold-out for telling people about Jesus. I was an average athlete in many different sports and had been a captain on several teams. I was sold-out for sacrificing in sports, and now I saw the same kind of sacrifice in Christians."

Brian was still cautious—and still hung up on his opinion of hypocrites—about this Christianity stuff.

"Then," Brian recalls, "someone said to me, 'People who go to church aren't saints. They're just sinners under construction.' I realized I needed to give my life to the Lord like I'd given it to sports. To sacrifice everything at the foot of the cross."

At age seventeen, he recommitted his life to the Lord.

After high school, he moved on to Houghton College and dedicated himself both to the Lord and to soccer. With Sports Ambassadors he saw how doors opened up, and he decided he wanted to be a soccer ambassador for the rest of his life.

Two events in college cemented his commitment to soccer as a means of spreading the gospel. One happened during his sophomore year.

"My dad and I were best friends," Brian says. "He came to all my games, both home and away. He was my greatest supporter. During my sophomore year, he died. I was with him that day. It was an incredible experience. I sang to him while he was in bed: 'Amazing Grace.' 'How Great Thou Art.' I was in the room with him when he actually took his last breath. It was as if God had just taken away my final safety blanket and my best friend."

The message in 1 Timothy 6:7 came to Brian. "You bring nothing into this world and you can't take anything out of it either. I realized one more time that I had to live my life for Jesus. I saw my dad—he took nothing with him. It was over. I saw that everything I did I had to do unto Him. Trophies and soccer balls weren't going to go with me. What would go with me would be the things that mattered to God."

The second event happened during his senior year. He was cocaptain of the soccer team. A goalkeeper. First string. A friend of his named Al Bushart, the other cocaptain, was late for practice one day. Somebody ran onto the field and handed the coach a note. He looked at it, turned the practice over to Brian, and left. Everyone wondered what was going on. Then one of the mothers arrived, desperately looking for her son. When she found him, she hugged him and wept.

"I ran after the coach, caught up to him, and asked what had happened. Al was my former roommate. We were both married at that point, and his wife was my wife's former roommate. In fact, he and his wife were coming to my apartment for dinner that night."

The coach told Brian there had been an accident. Six people were killed, including Al.

Brian gave up sports after that season. In 1982 he went to Puerto Rico to teach in a missionary high school. When the soccer coach quit, Brian was asked to take over. It was then that God gave Brian another dream.

"I wanted to put together a professional soccer team made up of Christians."

First, he coached a team involved with Sports Life, a forerunner of Missionary Athletes International (MAI). In 1987, he went with MAI and in 1990 started an East Coast ministry for them. With the different teams, Brian started traveling all over the world—Russia, Sweden, Germany, France, England.

They sponsored soccer camps for kids. Initially, the camps drew about 200 kids, but during Brian's stint, the camp grew to about 1,300 kids. A vision burned in his soul.

"When I played in high school and on church teams," he says, "I saw how some of the men would act. I had seen men really lose it on the field. Anger. Yelling. People mistreating people. In our camps, I wanted to teach kids not just how to be Christians and athletes, but how to be sports ministers. I wanted to show them how to conduct themselves as Christians. I emphasized sportsmanship and fair play and being obedient to the officials."

In 1992, Brian founded a pro soccer team called the Charlotte Eagles. Today, he is head coach of that team, which plays in the USISL (United States International Soccer League). The last two years they won the "Fair Play Award" for the league. They travel to over eighty cities playing pro teams and telling the good news.

So what was that great moment when Brian impressed his dad in his sophomore year in college?

It happened during the first game of the regionals.

"I always wanted to have a great experience that would impress Dad and my brothers," Brian says. "They were all athletes. Our house was full of trophies. So I wanted to do something incredible. Just once. Or maybe twice."

He was starting goalkeeper for fifteen of the sixteen games at Houghton that year. But he was benched going into the playoffs, during the regional tournament. "It was ironic, really. The whole season, I'd been telling the guys that you had to have the right attitude. 'Even when you're on the bench,' I told them, 'you've got to be committed to excellence and the team and everything.' Now I was benched and eating my own words. I was learning to live out what I'd been preaching.

"I was on the bench for the first game of the regionals. It went to the second round, final eight in the country. We were playing against Messiah College. Then our star player—the son of the coach—was injured. We were losing 1–0, twenty minutes to go. I had never played out in the field before, because I was always a goalkeeper.

"But Coach put me out in the field. I was in about five minutes playing right wing, one of three attacking players from the right side. There was a corner kick and the ball came at me. I was about twelve yards out from the goal. I'd never done a side volley in my life. That's when you receive a ball in the air while you're sideways and you lift your leg and kick it while it's in the air.

"The ball came at another player and he 'skip-headed' it off to me. It bounced. I got my foot up and side-volleyed it. It hit the inside of the back post. The goalkeeper, who was at the near post, rushed across. The ball ricocheted at him, struck his leg about two feet off ground, and went into the goal. It was incredible. I had scored the goal. The score was tied, 1–1."

The teams went into four overtimes trying to settle it. Brian says, "With a minute left to go in the fourth overtime, a friend dribbled down the left side of the field and beat several defenders. He crossed the ball from left flank in a pass to the front of the goal. I was running toward it, about twelve yards out. I had these black glasses on. The ball careened at me in the air and I headed it on my forehead. My glasses went flying up in the air. The ball ended up in the upper left corner of goal. One point! We won the game, 2–1, on the two goals I had made.

"My dad saw the whole thing. I'd done what I'd always wanted to do—an amazing feat [for me]—that he would remember. He died about three months later in February."

As coach of the Eagles, Brian frequently gives his testimony in places where the gospel would never be heard except for soccer.

"You know," he says, "in this country baseball and basketball and football are the biggest sports. But all over the rest of the world, it's soccer. Like I said, it opens doors. People will come to hear the gospel from a soccer player whom they'd never hear in a church service."

What a thrill to play a sport you love and to spread the news of the gospel! That's what Brian is doing and continues to do. It's a powerful platform and one with which the Lord must be immensely pleased.

★ Paul Zimmerman ★

Chapter 2

Height: 6 feet

Weight: 165 pounds

Position: Goalkeeper

Birth date: June 9, 1964

Team: **Charlotte Eagles**

Paul Zimmerman: Saved and Making Saves in the Goal

"**G**ood goalkeepers are born, not made."

So says Paul Zimmerman, one-time goalkeeper on two of Chicago's indoor soccer teams, the Chicago Sting and its minor league franchise, the Chicago Shockers. What he means is that hard work will only take you so far. You must possess special abilities to make it as a goalie. And, ulti-mately, only God can give you those.

Paul Zimmerman is one of these "born" goal-keepers. He's got grit, determination, commitment—and talent.

At age eight, Paul watched his older brother play soccer, and he took an interest in the game. Soon he enrolled in the Rochester Junior Soccer Club. There he launched himself as a goalkeeper, and he hasn't looked back since. He naturally fit into the position.

He comes from a soccer family. His parents bought season tickets to the Rochester Lancers, at that time an outdoor soccer club that played the New York Cosmos and other well-known teams. They went to every game and loved it.

Paul played goalie at East High School for four years and planned to go to college on a soccer scholarship, if possible. He even thought about becoming a pro back then, even though soccer had not taken hold very well in the United States.

But early in his senior season he broke his leg and was out for the year. Looking back, Paul says, "The Lord was putting me on the sidelines because soccer had become too big in my life." Like many soccer fanatics, Paul had allowed soccer to become the defining point of his life, and he knew God had to test that point. The first test was a broken leg.

I say "first" because another injury only a few

months later further challenged Paul's commitment both to soccer and to the Lord.

Paul was born and raised in a Christian home. He grew up believing in Jesus Christ and can't remember a time when he didn't believe. Sometimes that's good, and sometimes it's not so good. If someone becomes a believer at an early age, occasionally the fire grows cold in later years. There's no spark in the Christian life, and the person just plods along the path of Christian faith never really experiencing the great joy that it can bring.

On the other hand, believing early kept Paul away from many of the sins that others fall to. He remained committed to the Lord and steered away from the evils that can do a young man in. So he feels strongly that his life was greatly blessed by having Christian parents and believing early. But he's not one of those Christians who just plods along through life. He gives it his all and now revels in sharing his testimony at soccer games the world over.

The summer after Paul's senior year, the other disaster struck. His high school coach was taking an all-star soccer team on a tour of Germany that summer. Paul's leg had healed, he wanted to make the trip, and he worked twice as hard to get back into shape. He gave it his best shot and when time came for tryouts, he made the team.

It was a three-week tour involving twelve to fourteen games. Listen to what happened during the second game of the trip: "A defender and I were try-ing to clear the ball from the goal area. I slid out, div-ing after the ball at the defender's and an opponent's feet. The defender kicked me right in the jaw. Next thing I knew I was suffocating. I'd swallowed my tongue and I couldn't get any air. My coach reached in and pulled my tongue back out. I was alive, but it really hurt. My jaw was broken!"

That was another setback, and one that Paul thought might spell the end of soccer for him. He had wanted to go to a big soccer school—Indiana or St. Louis University, for example—but because of the broken leg they'd dropped him from consider-ation. And now the broken jaw. He worried that he wouldn't be able to continue on in a good program. However, Michigan State got interested, and he decided to go there. Although they had a middle-of-the-road program, they played some of the big pow-erhouses like Indiana, Akron, and St. Louis. Paul made the varsity his freshman year.

Still another tragedy struck Paul's life that he couldn't just leave behind. "After my freshman year my father died of cancer," he says. "He was my men-tor and biggest fan. I started asking the Lord what He wanted to do with my life. It was a tough time between injuries and Dad's passing. But the Lord showed me that I could use the gift of playing goalie to honor and glorify Him."

It was Paul's earthly father who directed him to his heavenly Father. Paul says, "When my father passed away after my freshman year in college, I knew that I really wanted to dedicate my life to the Lord. So that summer I was baptized in Canandaigua Lake, one of the Finger Lakes up there in New York State. I had never been baptized before. Christianity was all coming together and making sense in my life at that time."

Paul's father had been a church administrator and a true servant to the Lord. "His servant's attitude and mind-set were beautiful to see," says Paul. "Seeing my dad in his work and daily life—how he worked for God and not for man, honoring God in the daily concerns of life—was very influential. He was a church administrator. He could always be counted on to open up the church or have a room set up properly for different services. He would be there early in the morning or late at night to close up. He was very dedicated. He always worked to make sure the job was done properly."

Such an example of commitment to good work and excellence led Paul to give the same level of commitment to the Lord in his soccer playing. Over the next three years he played varsity soccer and excelled on a team that ranked in the middle among U.S. colleges. During his last two years he was selected as a regional all-American. He set school records for shutouts in one season (9) and in a career (29).

At the end of his senior year, he was invited to play in an East-West game called "The Budweiser Classic," at which indoor soccer coaches scouted the top players and selected the ones they wanted to try out for their teams. The Chicago Sting gave Paul the nod. He was the first goalkeeper taken in the draft, and the ninth pick overall.

The Sting played in the MISL (Major Indoor Soccer League), and their minor league team, the Chicago Shockers, played in the AISA (American Indoor Soccer Association). Paul spent most of his time shuttling back and forth between the Shockers and the Sting because he needed playing time. The Sting already had two veteran goalkeepers, but on the Shockers, Paul shone. In 1987, he was Rookie of the Year for the AISA.

Paul recognized it as a real honor, but he also realized there might not be much of a future for him with the indoor teams. He had felt a call to missions and considered going to Africa as a missionary with his family. He wanted above all to serve the Lord in soccer, and the environment he was in didn't lend itself to that. Few players in indoor soccer practiced Christian principles, let alone gave their lives to Christ. So Paul felt stymied.

In 1990 he got his first taste of using soccer as a means to missions. He toured with a team called the FC ("Football Club") Orange Seahorses, playing in Czechoslovakia and Poland. They would play a soccer game, then hold a rally and give testimonies. Often, players got into one-on-one ministering situations with opponents in the locker room. At the time, the Czechs were just emerging from almost half a century of communism, and they were very open to the Word. The Poles weren't quite at that stage yet, but the team was able to take Bibles into Poland and give them out. The Seahorses were a good team, winning about as many as they lost, but their purpose was ministry. It was ministering before thousands of people that turned Paul on.

Shortly thereafter, Paul and his wife traveled to Kenya in East Africa to serve as missionaries. They worked at a boarding school for missionary kids called the Rift Valley Academy. Paul coached the varsity soccer team, which played other boarding schools as well as the Kenyan schools, while his wife taught. But their primary responsibility was to a dorm full of twenty-two junior high boys. He worked with the kids, teaching them soccer skills and becoming kind of a surrogate parent for each of them.

Paul had two undefeated seasons at Rift Valley Academy—his first season and his last one. It was exhilarating for him to see kids develop and learn to play the game he loved.

This past year Paul played with the Charlotte Eagles, a team made up of Christians who consider themselves missionaries. "We raise support," Paul says, "and then play on the team, just like regular missionaries." Playing on a team of all Christians has been a wonderful experience for Paul.

He had only played a little bit in Kenya, practicing with high school boys, and looked forward to seeing if his skills were still there. The team ended up 14–6 this past year. In his first game with the Eagles, against Myrtle Beach, Paul made six or seven tough saves and intercepted seven or eight crosses in a 2–0 shutout. He played a good game and it appears he'll be a regular with the Eagles.

What's it like being a goalkeeper? For Paul it's the ultimate thrill—just one notch lower than giving his testimony and seeing people come to Christ. He says, "A goalkeeper feels tremendous pressure. You don't want to make a mistake. It's magnified in a goalie's case. If you slip up in the midfield, you can usually slough it off. But if you make a mistake in the goal box, everybody sees it."

According to Paul, the best goalkeepers don't reach their highest level until their late twenties or early thirties. Now thirty-one years old, Paul feels he's in his prime. "I'm better able to direct my defenders and take control of a game," he says. "The goalkeeper is usually the one to lead the others. By communicating with your defenders, how you distribute— pass the ball out from goal by punting or throwing— you control the game from a defensive standpoint. You are the first line of the offense, the one to make the first pass going forward. So goalkeeping is both an offensive and defensive position."

He believes the key element of goalkeeping is to give the field players the confidence that no goals will be scored during the game. A goalkeeper has to have the ability to make the big save when necessary.

Paul remembers one game during his Michigan State days against St. Louis University. "St. Louis was eighth-ranked in the country at the time," he says. "We were an underdog team coming to St. Louis. We took them by surprise and showed them we were someone to be reckoned with."

What happened? State scored a goal early in the first half, and Paul made a couple of key saves that kept St. Louis out of the net. One was on a one-on-one breakaway. The player, all alone, dribbled down the field toward Paul. Paul charged out to reduce the area in which the attacker could shoot. With a slide out in front of the player, he swiped the ball off the forward's foot and preserved State's lead. That was the same sort of play on which Paul broke his jaw years earlier, so it was a hair-raising move.

St. Louis tied the score in the second half. Then Michigan State came back and pumped in two more goals. Near the end of the game, Paul's team held off a furious rally. Then St. Louis got a penalty kick.

"In a penalty kick," Paul says, "it's the goalkeeper all alone against one offensive player, usually their best kicker. You can't move until the ball is actually touched by the kicker's foot. The goalie has to stand on the goal line and remain in position until the ball is finally touched. So you're standing there, sweating it out, knowing every face is fixed on you, and you have to try to guess and read the kicker as he approaches the ball. Eighty to ninety percent of penalty kicks score. So the odds are against you."

It was a tough moment. A score would bring St. Louis to within a goal of tying. Paul watched the kicker take position, then move toward the ball. He anticipated a low kick at the corner. In fact, almost all penalty kicks, when a good player is kicking, sail toward the corners, high or low.

Paul says, "You have twenty-four feet in which to maneuver. The goal box is eight feet high. On penalty kicks you typically try to put it one yard or less inside the posts."

That means if the goalie is at the middle of the goal line, the kicker has twelve feet to use on either side. "When you practice the penalty kick," he says, "you put a street cone inside the posts about one yard. You try to place the ball between the cone and posts.

"That was exactly where this kicker was going," Paul says. "The ball came in low. I dove to the left flat out, prone, stretching for all I was worth. The ball was less than a yard inside. A flawless kick. Somehow, though, I knocked the ball with my hands out away from the goal. It missed!"

It was a grand moment for Paul to stop a score that way. Most of the time the goalkeeper loses on penalty kicks, but this was one time when he won.

Paul says his Christian faith is key to his soccer playing. "I want to honor God through my ability. I don't seek to draw praise to myself. But like Eric Liddell said in *Chariots of Fire*, I want the spectators to sit back in awe and wonder at God, who has given us these abilities and gifts. When you make the spectacular save, you don't want it all to go to you. You want people to love the Lord for what He's done!"

Has Paul ever made a spectacular save?

"Yeah," he says. "This past summer in Greensboro, North Carolina, against the Greensboro Dynamo with the Charlotte Eagles. There was a volley from about ten yards away. It was a crossed ball. A guy had run downfield on the sideline and kicked the ball over to a man about ten yards out from the goal on the left-hand side. I had to go completely across the goal mouth to try and stop the guy from scoring. He kicked a side volley while the ball was still in the air. It headed for the upper left corner and I leaped toward that upper corner, got my hand on the ball, deflected it over the goal."

What tips does someone like Paul—both a player and a coach—give to those who would excel at goalkeeping?

"I emphasize repetitive catching of the ball off a board or wall. Do it four hundred to five hundred times at a practice so that it becomes second nature. Learn to catch all kinds of balls—over the head, in front, behind, straight on, diving, leaping. Stand in front of the board and throw. After you learn to catch everything and anything, you can go into the goal and let people kick the ball at you."

What about that depressing moment when the opposition scores against you? How does a goal-keeper handle that?

"If the other team scores, forget about it as soon as it happens. Go on to the next one. Always think of making a shutout. You have to be the first one to pick the ball up out of the goal. You have to send a message to your team, 'That's it. No more.'"

Paul keeps that philosophy on the field and in his life. It works the same way with sin as a Christian. If you commit a sin, confess it and forget it, then go on.

It's a sure bet Paul will continue to make his mark, both as a servant of Christ in stadiums all over the world, and as a servant in his home and church.

★ Desmond Armstrong ★

©Allsport

Height: 6 feet

Weight: 172 pounds

Positions: Defender,
Sweeper

Birth date: November 2,
1964

Team: **Charlotte
Eagles**

Desmond Armstrong: International Star

Soccer players are a breed apart, especially in the United States. They don't get attention like performers in football, basketball, baseball, and even hockey, and track and field. They're not well known, they don't get paid as well, and they don't make headlines like other sports people.

But they have heart.

Take Desmond Armstrong, one of America's most prominent soccer players. He has participated in over 84 international contests and once played for a Brazilian team called the Santos. He's played in the World Cup (1990) and for the U.S. Olympic team (1988). He has used his soccer ability as a platform for spreading the gospel of Christ.

He has heart.

Desmond started soccer at the ripe old age of eleven, when his family moved from Washington, D.C., where soccer was not a popular sport, out to Columbia, Maryland, which was soccer heaven. Soccer teams dotted the countryside like hairs on a hog's back, and Desmond picked up the game. He says, "The first two years I was pretty horrible. I had fun. But I was already eleven years old. That's kind of late for kids to start in soccer, especially in a soccer community like Columbia."

He went on to play striker and midfielder for Howard High School in Columbia, and for his last two years was voted MVP. He was also team captain and was named to all-county, all-metro, and all-state teams his final year. He led the team in goal scoring.

It was about that time that Desmond began thinking about soccer as a lifetime pursuit. He won a scholarship to the University of Maryland and played there all four years. Maryland performed poorly on the field and wasn't a contender, but Desmond was selected by the higher-ups for all-ACC (Atlantic

Coast Conference) honors three years in a row. He also made the all-South team two years.

But most of the excitement happened during his freshman year. He says, "We played against Duke. They were rated number one. We had tied them, 1– 1. It looked as though we would go on to be a con- tender. My most dramatic moment in college ball, certainly. We were young. No one knew us. The ball got served over to an Iranian player on my team. He kicked it hard, a nice straight shot. It went in. Two thousand people were watching it. The stands exploded! A wall of people surrounded the field. I was very happy!"

Although Maryland won that game, they didn't win many others that year. They just weren't a sea- soned, well-balanced team. But Desmond felt that he was on his way. He'd played in one big game, and he wanted more.

Out of college, Desmond was drafted by the Cleveland Force, for whom he played for the next three years.

Still, he doesn't especially like indoor soccer. "It was my first chance to play professionally," he says. "The only place to go. But I don't like it very much even though I made the all-star team my second year. It's a more physical game. You're confined. You can't jump away from tackles. You collide with other players constantly. It's almost like an ice hockey game. Lots of in-your-face stuff. And your reaction time is limited. You end up crashing into one another. It's fun for the spectators, but not for the player."

Even though indoor soccer is fun to watch for some, Desmond doesn't think it'll ever be really popular, with big names playing and lots of high-paying contracts. He says outdoor soccer requires much more strategy, much more finesse and endurance, much more commitment to the sport as a sport. International soccer, he says, is more fun to watch. Why?

"In the rest of the world, you have the best athletes playing soccer. Our best athletes are playing baseball, football, or basketball. But on an international team from Europe or South America or Africa, the whole team is all-stars. The play is much more physical. A much faster pace. The guys out there think faster, and they know what to do. They have an A plan, a B plan, a C plan. No matter who you play against, they're three steps ahead. It's a challenge."

Who does Desmond consider some of the best soccer players in the world?

"First, Marco Van Basten for Holland. He's a great player. Ruud Gullit, also of Holland, is amazing. And Bebeto for Brazil."

What makes these players such standouts?

"Marco knows how to think about the game. He's analytical about it. Ruud is six-two, 208 pounds. He's a phenomenal athlete. Bebeto is only about five-eight, but he's so quick, it's hard to stay with him."

Ruud Gullit played alongside Desmond at the World All-Star Game. "We were picked as all-stars and played on the same team," Desmond says. "I felt like I was playing with the very best athletes in the world, just as a basketball player would be amazed to play next to Michael Jordan."

One of the highlights for Desmond was playing in Brazil. "I had gone down to Brazil to play there and I played well. It was an awesome team. I learned a lot. But then I returned to the U.S. to play on the national team. We had a chance to play Brazil, my old teammates, in 1993. I wanted to prove to them I could compete. We ended up losing the game, 2–0. During the game, though, I caught the eye and attention of the Brazil coach. Afterwards, he told me I was a good player. I felt that was a real piece of recognition. I had reached an international level of play. That was important to me."

What are the marks of a good player according to Desmond Armstrong? "Dedication and a love for the game. A love for what we do. But it's dedication from the perspective that even when it's not fun, you're out there to improve yourself. Love for the game revolves around a desire and a will to play all hours of the day. You have to be dragged off the field. Mom has to call you home. That's what I'd call a real love for the game."

According to Desmond, the main strength of soccer is that it's the one international sport. No other game fills that place. Desmond says, "Soccer is the greatest sport in the world because no matter where you go in the world, you can get up a game of soccer. You can't say that about any sport. Why is soccer so popular? It's the poor man's sport. You just need a ball and you've got a game. You don't have to put up a hoop, or put on pads. Just go out there and kick."

How did Desmond become a Christian? His first year as a pro, he was thinking a lot about money and living by himself. His mom and dad were divorced, and now it was time to do his own thing. He began living a very loose, sinful life. He played defense for the Cleveland Force and the attention from the public was constant. He says, "A lot of women come after you. You go into training in the morning. Then you come home and watch soap operas in the afternoon if you don't have anything better to do. At night you go out with the boys, pick up women, and stuff like that. It seemed normal because everyone else was doing it.

"It got to a point where I went off the deep end. I was dating three or four girls at the same time. This was around the time of the 1988 Olympics. My personal life was going down the tubes. I was engaged to this Iranian girl. Her parents couldn't stand me. She wasn't really standing by me. That summer, I broke up with her.

"I went to the Olympics, competed, and came back. I began to take a long look at my life. What was

I doing—spinning wheels, getting diseases, spending all my money on junk? I had no inner peace. Then I ran into a college friend named Paul Hill. He invited me to his church. His family had always been Christian. When I went to church, I felt as if God's Word was talking directly to me. The pastor kept asking a certain question: Are you out there trying to do it by yourself? I said to myself, Yeah! I am!

"Then he had all the people pray. The pastor said, 'Do you need some help?' I sat there and it was like I was shouting it. Yeah! Yeah! YEAH! He said, 'There's someone who wants to help you. Are you willing to receive that help?' I said in my heart, 'Yes, I want to receive it.' So he said, 'Raise your hand if you want to do this.' I raised my hand. It didn't seem like much to ask.

"But then he said, 'For all of you who raised your hands, come down to the front.' I decided I wasn't going anywhere. This was getting embarrassing. But then an usher walked down and tapped me on the shoulder. They had people watching when we raised our hands. I felt on the spot, but something in me just said, 'Go down.' I got up and walked down the aisle. Since that time, I've been living for God."

After that experience, Desmond thought his life would all come together. But the strangest thing happened: two weeks later, he broke his leg. As he lay around the house recovering, he had a lot of time to think about himself, his beliefs, and soccer. Suddenly, he realized that he could survive without soccer if he had to. God would provide for him.

"For a long time," Desmond says, "soccer was it for me. It was my God. I believed I could make all my money playing soccer. When I got saved, it changed my whole perspective on soccer and life. With God, I had a direction. I wanted to serve Him. Now with the platform He's given me, I can really see how He's leading. My life is a testimony to others. People will pay attention to soccer, and through soccer to a Christian testimony."

Desmond's soccer success has put him in the public eye in more ways than one. There's a sports Bible called *The Path to Victory Bible*. In it, you can read the stories of many sports personalities, including Desmond's. But guess who's pictured on the front cover of the Bible? You got it—Desmond Armstrong. It's been a means for him to spread the news of the gospel.

He says, "A friend noticed my picture on the cover of that Bible. He started calling me for advice. He wanted to know about God. He knew I was a Christian. He felt he was at a crossroads.

He just wanted to talk about Jesus. So I told him about having a personal relationship with God through Jesus.

"He came to our early morning prayer at church and the word that was preached talked about a need to have God in your life, especially when times are tough. After we finished praying, this friend asked the head pastor to pray over him. The pastor asked him, 'Are you saved?' He wasn't sure. So they prayed together, and he made the commitment.

"He's done wonderfully since then. He comes to church consistently. He reads the Word every day. He's growing. Taking a different look at life now. All he wanted to do was be a pro and make money playing soccer. He realizes now there might be a different calling on his life. He's waiting on God."

Still other people have been influenced by Desmond's life through his involvement with soccer.

"Two close friends on the Washington Warthogs knew about my commitment," Desmond says. "They noticed that I was living differently from many soccer players. I was married, I had two kids and a home. These two guys wanted to change. They thought the Lord was the only way to put them on the right path."

Desmond has had some real ups and downs playing soccer. In 1988 he played on the Olympic team. Then in 1990, he performed in the World Cup. Even though the United States didn't get past the first round, Desmond put in one of his best efforts.

He got noticed. People interviewed him and he had many chances to share his faith.

But Desmond was cut from the 1994 World Cup team. Desmond says, "I started a Bible study in my house for the team players. The coach didn't believe in God or in the Bible. He thought it made you weak, so he prohibited it. But I continued to meet with the players, encouraging them and praying with them. The coach saw us praying before a game, something we always did. He walked over and yelled at us to stop.

"I've played in eighty-four international games. I'm number five in games in the U.S. for the past seven years. Up to that point I was starting every game. But this new coach just didn't seem to like me. I got interviewed by quite a few newspapers. Then it came to a head. I didn't do a lot of team activities.

"For instance, there was this wet T-shirt contest at a local bar. The coach encouraged us to go. I and Hugo Perez didn't go. The next day, the coach arrived back at the clubhouse. He told Hugo and me that we missed it. First thing that came to my mind was, I have a wife. So I said to him, 'What does your wife think about that?' It was uncalled-for, I guess. I shouldn't have said it. He was very miffed. He didn't say anything. But after that there was a genuine dislike for me. He was intent on getting rid of me. So he cut me."

Getting cut bore the seeds of a real disaster. Desmond and his family were living on barely nothing at the time, and now he was out of a job. But the same day he received his walking papers, he called ABC and other news organizations to see if they wanted him to commentate at the World Cup. Five days later he got a job.

Desmond served as a studio analyst beside Jim McKay, the famous Olympics commentator. It turned out that Jim McKay didn't know much about soccer. So Desmond filled the airwaves with his thoughts on what the teams were doing right or wrong, where they were going, who might win, and so on. Desmond got rave reviews. *USA Today* named him "Rookie of the Year." And he got more jobs, including one for ESPN. For a whole year he's been able to get work as a television personality and commentator.

"God is faithful," Desmond says. "I could have been devastated from being cut for the World Cup. It was in the U.S. that year. What a chance to excel and say something for the Lord. Now that opportunity was gone. But it's been a pure blessing. ABC is the top, and I went straight to the top. I can only be thankful for what God is doing."

Maybe Desmond ought to be a preacher! He says, "If you have faith in our Lord Jesus Christ, He will always stand by you. That's Romans 8:38–39. I'm not out there on my own. God can do all things and He'll always stand by you. We have two kids and we're expecting a third. We're keeping things together by a shoestring. This past year or two has proven, though, that God is there. For those out there going through tough times, no matter what, God is there beside you."

Another problem that struck recently proves the same point. Desmond played two games for the Charlotte Eagles, a Christian pro team. He loved it. The team competes at a high level, but the fellowship and the sharing of the gospel with opponents is the main thing.

Then he returned to Maryland to play indoor soccer for the Washington Warthogs. The first week, he got injured—hurt his knee—and went into rehabilitation. He says, "The team management began to grumble that I was being paid but wasn't playing. Basically, they wanted to take my money away. So I said, 'Okay, that's all right. God's in charge.'"

When the team released him, Desmond worried what he'd do for an income. But once again, God provided. "The next day I thought of a company I knew of called Precepts Sports and Entertainment. I knew the owner and had driven past his office. Something in me said, 'Call him.' So I called. He said, 'You couldn't have called at a better time.' He does mostly basketball. Another guy does football. He needed someone to do soccer."

Desmond ended up getting a whole sales division for himself. He knew it was God watching out for him.

"With this company, I do camps, speaking engagements, games. I'll design camps on behalf of clients. I'll seek endorsements for clients. We help manage their careers. I don't know what God's doing, but He has me there for a reason."

It seems that nothing happens to these Christian soccer players that doesn't make sense from a divine point of view. God does strange things. One of the strangest is how you make friends and build relationships in soccer that last for years.

When Desmond was fifteen, he played on a regional eastern team during a tournament. Another player named Scott Cook (also in this book) witnessed to Desmond one night. He sashayed into Desmond's room and shared the gospel with him. It was Desmond's first encounter with Christ. He didn't become a Christian then, but Scott had planted a seed that would yield fruit several years later.

And last year, Scott played with Desmond for the Charlotte Eagles!

It's a small world.

But God is doing great things. And if you listen to Desmond Armstrong, you can be sure the same kind of great things will happen to you if you follow Him.

☆ Philip Wolf ☆

©1995 by Cindy Skop

Chapter 4

Height: 5 feet, 9 inches

Weight: 170 pounds

Position: Midfielder

Birth date: February 28, 1970

Team: **Charlotte Eagles**

Philip Wolf: Following Caleb

Do any biblical characters come to your mind when you think of soccer?

Not many come to mine. Soccer wasn't around in Bible times. But Phil Wolf regards Caleb as his favorite Bible figure. He was the man who wanted "that mountain" when he was over eighty years old, the second of the two spies who said Israel could take the land when the other ten said they couldn't.

Phil wrote Caleb's name on his soccer shoes every time he played. Why? As an encouragement.

But that's getting ahead of the story.

"I wanted to play pro soccer since the age of ten," Phil Wolf says. "It was a dream. Actually, I started out liking basketball. But my older brother got into soccer. His junior year in high school he brought home an all-conference plaque. That was enough for me. I quit playing basketball and dedicated myself to soccer. I played for club teams and against my brother and his friends. We had a lot of pickup kind of games. I played my first official soccer game in seventh grade. A club team."

That's the way it starts for many pro soccer players. They begin when they're eight, nine, ten, and the dream sticks. They play for clubs, neighborhood teams, sometimes a traveling team. They learn the basic moves. They work out, get in shape, learn to run steadily for an hour and a half in a game. They get the "eye of the tiger," as a movie once put it. They learn to lose, win, and tie.

It's pretty much a standard story. And Phil Wolf is right in the middle of it. It's funny how many of the soccer players in this book had older brothers who got them interested in the sport. Older brothers have that special zap for younger ones. But it's the younger ones who go on into the pros.

How come?

No one knows. Maybe God made us that way!

For Phil, it all started to come together in high school. "In high school I played midfield," he says. "I was the first freshman to start on the high school varsity, playing forward. I had some good years there. During my last two years I played center midfield. It was a lot of fun. I managed to set career scoring and assist-leader records in high school. For my last three years I was first-team all-conference. I didn't get all-state my senior year. That was a disappointment. But I began to realize the difference between serving the Lord and winning awards."

What does he mean? Just this: in soccer you can win all the awards but still lose your soul. The Lord is the center of Phil's life. He doesn't remember a time when he didn't believe in Jesus. His father is a professor of Old Testament at Wheaton College, one of the best-known Christian colleges in the United States. His family attended church from the time he was born, so he simply grew into it. His Christian values have kept him out of a lot of trouble, he says, because he might have gotten swept up in the whole sports personality thing fed by the press and the media. It could have messed him up. But Jesus kept him on course.

Playing at Wheaton College was a great opportunity for Phil, as it would be for any young man. Wheaton is a Division III school and plays teams like Ohio Wesleyan, Seattle Pacific (Division II), University of Wisconsin-Oshkosh, and Washington University in Missouri. There are no athletic scholarships in Division III. While there, Phil played every game all four years and was a three-time all-American.

By the way, what is this all-American thing we keep hearing about? This is the way it works: Every year in each of soccer's three divisions, three teams of eleven guys—nine teams altogether—are chosen for their excellent play. Each division has a first-team all-America, second-team all-America, and third-team all-America. The first team are the very best players at each position for that division—the cream of the crop of soccer players in America.

Phil was second team for Division III his sophomore year and first team his junior and senior years.

His first year at Wheaton he played sweeper, his second two years center midfield, and his last year forward. He finished third in Wheaton history in career scoring and set the school's career assist record.

"My junior year," Phil says, "we got to the final four. My brother had won a national championship in 1984, so I wanted to equal that. However, we lost to Ohio Wesleyan in the semifinals, 1–0. We ended up in third place that year."

Still, Phil had some great games during that time. One of the best came against Messiah College, rated number five in the East in Division III at the time. The game was played on Messiah's home field, and about three thousand people filled the stands. As Phil tells it, "Messiah controlled the game.

We were outmatched. But at one point we got down to their goal. I headed a throw-in to another player, who kicked it in. Score. I also assisted on the second goal. Both of them were kind of weird—what I call 'ugly goals.' But we won, 2–0. It was great!"

Out of college Phil was drafted in the second round by the Chicago Power. A friend named Bret Hall played on the team. It turned out to be a hard transition for Phil, who had come from Wheaton where they support you on the team and pray with you. At Chicago he had a tyrant of a coach.

"It was bad," Phil says now. "The ball almost became square instead of round for me. I couldn't kick it any which way and give it real direction. I had no confidence. I couldn't control the ball. It was because the coach was always bearing down on me. I'd never come across that in my life."

Stop and think about that. Here is an excellent soccer player and enthusiast who is finally living his dream—playing in the pros. But he has a nasty coach. No, not just nasty. A tyrant.

A coach makes a big difference. He can bring out the best in you if he works it right, and he can bring out the worst. For Phil, this coach was no help. He dragged the fellow down. He made him feel like nothing.

That's not the way to coach. If you have a man leading you who is like that, you might want to think about another team. Leaders don't lead by bashing you over the head. They lead by encouraging, guiding, helping, strengthening. If that's not happening for you, consider what Phil did.

"A friend named Scott Cook [he's also in this book] called me from Dayton where he played for the Dynamo. He said a Christian had bought the team—Dick Chernesky—and they were looking for Christian players. That was enough for me. I asked for my release from the Power and headed to try out for the team in Dayton."

And suddenly the ball became round again. "The first time I got out there and did something right, the coach, Terry Nicholl, said, 'Good job.' Immediately, I knew I was in the right place, and in a matter of days I became a better player than I was in Chicago."

What's it like to play on a team with other Christians? For Phil it was heaven, the fulfillment of a dream he'd always had. Initially, there were two Christians besides Phil on the Dayton Dynamo. Those three became little evangelists within the team and within the league. Soon six or seven on a roster of about eighteen players were Christian. Scott Cook was the pioneer, and Phil was the supportive midfielder!

They instituted chapel services led by a chaplain before every game. Eight or nine guys would come to the meetings, where the chaplain would share something motivational out of God's Word. "It was only about fifteen minutes," Phil says. "It was always well before the game. I remember for a long time I had a real fear of failure. One night the chaplain shared his lesson from the life of Caleb. He talked about how Caleb was this mighty warrior who served God wholeheartedly. He retold the story of the twelve spies, how Joshua and Caleb stood alone, saying God would help Israel conquer the land. They lost that battle, but God rewarded Caleb and Joshua years later.

"So I started to write 'Caleb' on my shoes. No matter how good the opponent was, no matter how many all-stars, I knew I could face down the giants. I kind of looked at great players in our league as giants, I guess, but with people like Caleb to encourage me, I knew that I could perform because the Lord was with me."

You might never think of Caleb as a soccer player, but he set a fine example for at least one fellow on the Dayton Dynamo.

Like many of the players in this book, Phil prefers outdoor soccer to the indoor variety. He says, "Indoor is crazy. It's much faster, much more random. You usually have a very high scoring game. It's exciting to watch, but I don't think there's as much skill or finesse involved."

In indoor soccer today you can score three kinds of goals. The highest point-counters are three-point goals, which must be shot from behind the 45-foot mark. Regular goals are worth two points, and one point is awarded for goals in shootouts or after penalties for serious fouls. In such a case, a player goes one-on-one with the goalie. He starts at the penalty goal line and has five seconds to shoot. If he scores, it's one point. One point is also awarded for power-play goals, when five players go against four.

Of course, in outdoor soccer there are eleven men on each team—one goalie and ten players. In indoor soccer, there are only six men on each team, one goalie and five players.

Phil says, "The three years I spent in Dayton were tough. We had a talented team. We were 20–20 after the first year. But then we went 16–24 the next two years. We didn't make the playoffs any of the years I was there."

The greatest thing about the Dynamo for Phil was playing with other Christians. Phil even saw several players become Christians during his time there.

"One of the hardest players I've ever played with was on that team," he says. "He tackled hard. He could really make you hurt. He grew up in the inner city, Los Angeles, a tough kid. One night we went to an Easter celebration and invited this tough player to come along. At the church, they performed a cantata, acting out the story of Christ, His crucifixion and resurrection. We were all deeply moved by the service. But when it came time for the gospel message, this tough guy raised his hand to receive Christ.

"After that, he didn't change in his outward behavior. He was still a tough soccer player. But he softened toward us as Christians. He was very open. He began reading the Bible and would talk to us on bus trips."

Playing with other Christians was an answer to Phil's most fervent prayer. "I'd wanted to be a pro my whole life. In Chicago, I lost it. My dream was gone. Things didn't work out. That coach just scared me and ruined me. But then I went to Dayton and it was a miracle. All the guys on the team were impacted greatly for Christ."

Phil's philosophy of life, soccer, and Christian faith comes down to this: "God's given us certain abilities for work or play. God gifted people to play soccer, too. I knew from the earliest age that was what I wanted to do. God has blessed those desires. The most important thing to me is my relationship with the Lord. I'm not out there trying to play for money or the fans or my parents or a girlfriend. I'm just trying to glorify the Lord by what I do."

What advice would Phil give to those who would excel in soccer? "The most important thing is setting your mind on doing soccer. You have to put in hours and hours of time learning to dribble and kick. You have to set your mind to the hard work.

"Above all, you must get really familiar with the soccer ball. You have to learn to control it. Learn to juggle—keep the ball in the air with your feet, your thighs, your head. I always heard from soccer players and coaches that the 'soccer ball is your best coach.' Get to know the soccer ball, how you control it with your chest and thighs. Touch it as many ways and times as you can."

As a Christian, though, Phil sees something else: "You play the game to have fun. You don't have to be a pro or a college player. If the Lord has gifted you in this area, let God lead you. Sports nowadays has too much pressure. If you don't love the game, do something else. Have fun. Enjoy it. If you're not having fun, it's useless."

Phil has great hopes for soccer in the United States. This coming year, a group of investors and players are starting up Major League Soccer (MLS), a major league just like in baseball, football, basketball, and hockey. They'll start with ten teams, bring in World Cup players, and pay legitimate money. It'll be the league people have been wanting for years.

Phil says, "I'd like to do that if I could. There are maybe two hundred jobs available. If the Lord wants me in the league, I'll be there."

And maybe you'll be rooting for him.

☆ James Wellington ☆

Height: 5 feet, 10 inches

Weight: 175 pounds

Position: Forward

Birth date: August 22, 1973

Team: **Charlotte Eagles**

James Wellington: The Goal Maker

What is the most goals you've scored in one game? One? Two? Three?

Let me tell you about a guy who made even more than that.

Jamie Wellington's older brother hurt his knee playing football when he was in the sixth grade, and his mother refused to let him play football anymore.

She felt it was too rough for kids. But she wanted him to get into good physical condition, so he turned to soccer.

When Jamie saw his brother, who was four and a half years older, out there on the field, kicking the ball, dribbling, finessing the defenders, he got interested. He wanted to be like his brother. So he played soccer, too.

Mom was happy. Brother was happy. Jamie was happy.

All that happiness! See what soccer can do for a family?

Truly, though, when a family gets involved in a sport that teaches skills, fosters self-reliance and teamwork, and builds up a person, it has to be a good thing. For Jamie that is precisely what soccer did. He loved it.

That first year he got involved on a YMCA team. As he moved up through the ranks and on through the years, he played in an outdoor travel league for the same YMCA. By the time he reached seventh grade, he was playing year-round—indoor in the winter, and outdoor in the fall, spring, and summer.

By tenth grade, though, Jamie found he preferred outdoor soccer to indoor. "Indoor soccer is very hard on your body," Jamie says. "It's not as much fun as outdoor. Indoor is more a game of speed and quickness. Outdoor's much slower. Players are just as fast, but there's much more room to work." Even today he's not much interested in indoor soccer, and has confined his efforts to the outdoor game.

In high school Jamie played three years on varsity as a defender and midfielder for Orchard Park High School in Orchard Park, New York. "We did well, had a good team," he says. "But we lost in the sectional finals in the tournament. Both my sophomore and senior years we lost."

One thing that has always stuck with Jamie is a little moment of failure in one of those sectional finals. When he was a sophomore, he missed a penalty kick. "It's always been a burden for me," he says. "It was a big chance. I've had many successes in soccer, but that miss still nags at me."

That's not to say Jamie is not a goal maker. He went on to play for four years at Houghton College, where soccer is a big sport and the most successful sports program at the school. As a freshman midfielder he scored sixteen goals and made honorable mention all-American—quite an achievement for a freshman.

His sophomore year set him back a bit. He hurt his ankle and wasn't mobile enough to play midfielder, so the coach moved him back to sweeper. Still, offense was his love. He scored eight goals that year and was an honorable mention all-American once again.

In his junior year big things started to happen. The coach moved him up to forward and installed a new system that was so much better Houghton racked up an 18–2–1 record. Jamie scored 29 goals, eclipsing by 9 the school record of 20. His record-breaking twenty-first goal was his first playoff goal and came in the districts at home. The crowd went wild, and Jamie received the game ball as a result. "Sort of put that one penalty kick miss to shame," he says. He also made third-team all-American that year.

For his senior year Houghton took on a new coach. The team excelled again, going 20–3, and Jamie scored 44 goals, was a first-team all-American, and played in the Umbro Senior Classic, an all-star game for seniors across the country. East versus West. Jamie's team won, 2–0.

The real drama came in the regional finals against Bloomfield College of New Jersey. Both teams put in a solid performance, but at the end of the second half, the score was 1–1. They had to go into overtime.

"I dribbled down the field in the overtime, and one of the defenders stole the ball from me about twenty-five yards out from goal," Jamie says. "I chased him and shot in on his blind side. Sliding in for the tackle, I took the ball away from him. He was so surprised I was there that he almost stopped running. I got well out ahead of him, though, and dribbled in. One defender flailed out at me. I evaded him and ran around him. Then another defender tried to take me out. I dribbled past him."

He felt like he was running on premium. Jamie eluded everyone Bloomfield threw at him. "Then the goalie ran out, trying to snuff me. I had about half the goal to shoot at. The goalie ran at me, but I kicked."

Shoot.

Score.

Game over! Wellington got the winning goal.

He says, "It was so great, because my whole family was there—Mom, Dad, my two brothers, and two of my three sisters. This was the last game that I would play at Houghton. And because we won, we went on to nationals where, unfortunately, we lost both of our games in group play."

Houghton made it a contest, though. In the first game, Houghton lost to Incarnate Word College, 5–4, with Jamie contributing three goals. Then they lost the second, 7–5, to Lindsey Wilson College. Again, Jamie racked up three more beauties and kept his name, if not his team, on the charts.

"There was a lot of excitement, though, in an earlier game," Jamie says, referring to a regular season game. "We were down, 3–0, in the first twenty minutes. We just kept playing, and got back up to 4–4. To come back from 3–0 was a big accomplishment for us. Then our other forward corner-kicked it to me. He was great for me to play with. A great passer. Good at setting me up. He corner-kicked it and two players, one from each team, stood in the way. I thought the ball was too high for them, though, and I was right: they didn't get it. I side-volleyed the shot on the fly. It went into the goal. And we won."

How did Jamie become a Christian?

It happened in the summer between his sophomore and junior years in high school. A fellow he played soccer with in high school called him up one day. They were friends, but Jamie didn't normally hang around with him. Actually, he was surprised this guy called him. They talked on the phone and this fellow asked Jamie what he was doing that day. Jamie said, "Nothing in particular."

The friend said, "I have a friend I want you to meet."

That day, two Young Life leaders came over to Jamie's house. They didn't talk about Jesus or anything religious but simply hung out. "We swam at our pond," Jamie says, "and hung around my house. They were just living out their Christian walk. They didn't want to scare me off, I guess. But then we hung out the next day. They wanted to build a friendship 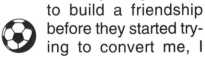 before they started trying to convert me, I

suppose. Young Life works hard at building friend-
ships before sharing the gospel."

That same week, on a Sunday, the two coun-
selors asked Jamie if he was busy the coming week.
"How would you like to come to Young Life camp?"
one of them asked.

"I kind of shrugged," Jamie says. "I didn't know
anything about it. But then one of the leaders told
me, 'If it isn't the best week of your life, I'll give you
your money back.'

"That amazed me, so I went. And it was a great
week. The people there, from the counselors to the
campers to the staff, were nice, friendly, and made
me feel very welcome. I didn't have to do anything to
impress them. Just the fact that I was there made
them take an interest in me. That was totally different from what I was familiar with. In high school you
always had to do something to impress your friends.
I used sports as a way to impress people. But there,
at Lake Saranac in upstate New York, I felt the
Christians at this camp cared about me for who I
was rather than what I was.

"Every night they had a speaker. Each night he
went through the steps necessary for the salvation
plan. Each night built until Thursday where they told
me about Christ being resurrected and everyone
can know Him and be saved. It made so much
sense to me. I thought, *If that's true, there's no
sense in me not going after it right now.*

"I sat and talked to the two Young Life coun-selors—Mike Maisel and Eric Segool—for about two hours on Friday. They prayed with me. Later that night we had what they call a 'Say So.' Anyone who had made a commitment to Christ stands up and says they've trusted Christ. So when it came time, I stood."

After becoming a Christian, sports didn't seem as important to Jamie as they had been. He still wanted to win, but it wasn't the ultimate thing for him. His con-version didn't effect too dramatic a change at first. After all, he was your basic decent kid. But he real-ized there was a higher purpose to things. His family wasn't a real churchgoing group, but after the Young Life camp, he started attending church regularly.

After high school, he wanted to go to a big school like Ohio State or the University of Buffalo. But when he visited those campuses, he didn't feel comfort-able or accepted there. Then he visited Houghton. "I felt really comfortable there," he says now. "And people made me feel extremely welcome. I was the first one from my immediate family who went there."

It was during his college days at Houghton that Jamie had his highest scoring game ever.

"It was bad weather that day. Raining. Windy. Cold. We were playing at St. John Fisher College in Rochester, New York. Before the game I actually felt sick, a little flu or something. It wasn't until late in the second half that I really started to come on and feel better. The first two goals I hardly remember. They passed by in a blur because I felt so sick. We were ranked pretty high in the country at the time. In the top ten. It was a big game for us. Their players were loud, yelling, swearing, nasty. Calling us wimps and stuff like that. The crowd was yelling at us, too. They said we were nothing in the rain, and individually we didn't have any talent—in so many words, if you get my meaning.

"I remember hitting the crossbar a few times. I kicked at the goal probably eight or nine times that day.

"Then in the second half with ten minutes to go, I remember getting the ball out in front of the bench and hearing from the sidelines, 'He has nothing. He's no one. Take the ball away from him.' I wanted to prove something, even though I'd already scored two goals. So I gritted my teeth and dribbled down toward their goal. On the way, I beat a few defenders, then shot. We scored. That calmed the crowd down a bit. People were double-teaming me, but I wasn't really thinking about it.

"My fourth goal that day was similar to the third. I took the ball about forty yards from the goal. Beat a couple defenders. Shot at around ten yards. Goalie was coming out. The ball ripped past him. A piece of cake."

His fifth—mark that, *fifth goal in one game*—was a penalty kick.

"The crowd was really screaming now. But I stood at the line and the goalie looked at me like, 'I'm not gonna let you beat me this time.' I figured I'd go for one side or the other. Ran up. Swatted it. The goalkeeper leaped to his left. But I kicked it to his right. It went in. Game over, 5–1."

Jamie had scored all five of his team's goals, almost single-handedly. Amazing.

What tips might he give a future goal scorer? "The hardest shot for a goalie to save is low. It's harder for him to get down on the ground. His hands are already up in the air. Shoot for the corners. That's the way to score goals."

This past year, Jamie played forward for the Charlotte Eagles, scoring 14 goals in twenty games. He also worked at several soccer camps in Charlotte, Boston, Tennessee, and Atlanta.

And the future?

"My main goal now is to teach," he says. "I'm not sure what grade or what level. I'd like to coach, but I don't know where. Right now I'm just finding myself. I'm a graduate assistant coach at the University of Mobile. I'm doing graduate work in education.

"My future in soccer? I'd like to play as long as I can, probably back in Charlotte, for the Eagles. I would like to coach some day, too. We'll see."

Keep your eyes open. You may be seeing Jamie Wellington out there on the turf, beating defenders and making goals.

"Major League Soccer is something I've thought about," says Jamie. "If I get an opportunity, I'll probably go out for it."

And the goal-maker will probably make it.

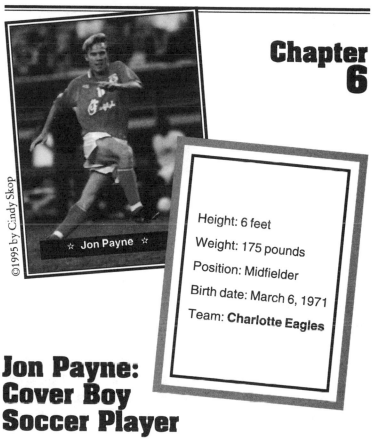

©1995 by Cindy Skop

☆ Jon Payne ☆

Height: 6 feet

Weight: 175 pounds

Position: Midfielder

Birth date: March 6, 1971

Team: **Charlotte Eagles**

Chapter 6

Jon Payne: Cover Boy Soccer Player

Sports Illustrated—the Bible of the sports world. It covers every major sports event the world over, and many minor ones. It exalts some personalities, and shows the mistakes of others. For Jon Payne, being in Sports Illustrated was a highlight of his soccer career.

Jon started playing at seven years old when his dad signed him up for a local team. Spring soccer. Low key. Jon ended up falling in love with the sport and, that year, was selected MVP by his teammates.

Sports occupied a huge spot in his life. His dad worked as a sportswriter for the *San Jose Mercury-News*, and also free-lanced for *Soccer America*. So sports always took up a large part of Jon's time and afternoon play. The first word he ever said was "ball."

When Jon turned eight years old, he tried out for a select traveling team that ended up winning the state championship that year. About a dozen of the guys from that team ended up going to college on scholarships. All the teams he played for were very successful.

And the successes just kept piling up. One year, in an under-fourteen tournament called the Friendship Cup, he participated on a higher level than ever before. Over one hundred teams from all over the world played in this international tournament. It was held in Denver, Colorado, that year. His team made it to the final, and Jon scored three goals. *Sports Illustrated* featured a picture of him with a little blurb about the game. What a high mark for him!

But it was only the beginning.

After that stellar year, Jon played on a number of teams that led to him making the national team for players under age seventeen. By the time Jon was a sophomore in high school, his team qualified for the under-seventeen World Cup and traveled to Honduras for a month. They played Honduras, Trinidad and Tobago, Costa Rica, and Mexico, and ended up qualifying for the final against Mexico.

The average crowd at the stadium was from 30,000 to 40,000 people. The game aired on national television in Honduras, and the commentators gave Jon a nickname—El Rubio—which means, "the blond." Jon was the only blond guy in the whole tournament.

Perhaps the biggest game of his life happened against Costa Rica. His team was down, 1–0, with ten minutes to go. Jon stood on the sidelines and hurled the ball in to a teammate, who headed the ball back to Jon. Jon then spun past a defender and sent up a cross. The ball whizzed across the front of the goal and one of his teammates skimmed it with his head. It went into the goal.

But that wasn't the highlight, although it did mean an assist for Jon. Toward the end of the game, one of his teammates crossed a ball in front of the net and another teammate headed it directly toward the goal. But it didn't go in. It struck the crossbar and bounced back out. Jon whipped in from the side and headed it back into the goal.

Score!

Jon didn't play soccer his first two years in high school because the team wasn't that good. He played basketball. But then he decided he had to contribute to his alma mater and joined the soccer team. He ended up being named Gatorade State Player of the Year and an all-American. Also, *Parade Magazine* made him a national all-American. He scored over 20 goals both years.

Another highlight occurred the summer between high school and college when he was asked to play for the West team in the Olympic Sports Festival. The team consisted of some pretty big-name players that year, men who would go on to become household names in Europe and South America: Cobi Jones, Mike Lapper, Joe Max-Moore, and Chris Henderson. Every day Jon awakened with a new sense of awe that he was playing in this tournament with these guys.

Jon scored five goals, the most in the tournament. Three of them came in the final against the East. He says, "I don't really remember the goals. Now it's a blur. I was just there. It happened fast. Kick. In. Kick. In. Kick. In. Like that. The game was on ESPN that night. I was named MVP of the tournament."

He adds, "It's probably the best I've ever played in my life."

Such games are rare for most soccer players. Once-in-a-lifetime affairs. So Jon learned to savor those moments.

He went on to Clemson University, one of the top soccer colleges in the country, always in the top ten. Jon started all four years and was named to the sec-

 ond-team all-ACC twice. Clemson won the ACC championship his sophomore year, 1990, and was ranked number one in the country, but lost in the playoffs, 3–0, to Scott Cook's team, the University of South Carolina.

It was in college that Jon was snapped awake in a very dramatic way. He says, "I was in a drunk-driving accident. I was driving. Up until that point, I was living an extremely worldly life—drinking and drugs and all that. I cracked the car up and was thrown in jail. Fortunately, no one was hurt.

"Up until that time, I always had a belief in Jesus and God, but it was never personal. That night I felt more scared than I've ever been. And that same night God came to me in my cell as I sat there. It was an overwhelming knowledge of my sin and of Jesus being the Savior. I went through a grievous time of repentance, realizing I was a sinner and my life amounted to nothing even in the midst of all my awards and popularity and fame. I knew I had to surrender my life to the Lord because he was truly what life was all about."

It caused a stunning turnaround in Jon's life. A couple of short months after that, God called him into full-time ministry. He realized that he wanted to teach the Bible and share the gospel, with young people especially. He longed to go into high schools and churches and places like that to tell young people what had happened to him, and that it could happen to anyone, anywhere, anytime.

That doesn't mean, though, that he has forgotten his soccer days and what soccer meant to him. He says, "I never thought I'd play soccer again when I hung up my boots after college. But then Brian Davidson of the Eagles visited me at Clemson, telling me that they were a pro team, but they were Christians who wanted to share the gospel through soccer. That intrigued me.

"I moved to Charlotte after I graduated in December 1993 and played for the Eagles. I also started a full-time job at Christ Covenant Church as a full-time senior high youth pastor."

Playing for the Eagles has been a great experience for Jon, building bridges with hundreds of people. Working with children in camps and clinics gave him a wonderful feeling of hope and fulfillment. Seeing so many people receive the message of Christ motivates him like nothing else.

"I was named Atlantic Division All-Star the last two years with the Eagles," Jon says. "But these last two years soccer has not been as significant in my life. The greatest thing I remember from it all is sharing with so many of my friends in the pro leagues about my faith.

"For instance, one conversation happened this past year after a game. I sat down with a player and we made some small talk. I asked him what he thought about our team and the gospel and who he thought Jesus was. As we talked, his whole face changed. We entered a very sincere conversation about the gospel and his life. Afterwards, I gave him a Bible and we hugged—something that rarely happens in soccer, especially with an opponent."

Still, that wasn't the highest point of all.

"This past year, my dad came to watch several of my games with Charlotte and stayed out here ten days. I had been sharing the news about Jesus with him and praying for him for about four years. The last night we were together, God led me to be up front with him about the state of his soul."

Jon and his dad went out to dinner. "I confronted him on where he stood with Jesus," says Jon. "It came down to the fact that he believed in Jesus and believed He had risen from the dead, but he had never made a commitment to serve Him. At the end of the meal, I asked him if he wanted to pray. He did. And he prayed to receive Jesus in his heart. It was definitely one of the most exciting days of my life."

Unfortunately, Jon doesn't see himself playing soccer much longer. He recently returned from a trip to Ecuador with Mission to the World, a Presbyterian agency. In Ecuador, he worked in a home for street children, helped two Presbyterian church's that were just getting started, and also worked with the Quichua Indians. Jon speaks Spanish fairly fluently. They offered many vacation Bible school kinds of activities for the kids, and Jon also led several soccer clinics.

So what happened?

"Through it all," Jon says, "the Lord called me to full-time Christian service over there. I'd been thinking a lot about what God has wanted me to do. I've traveled all over the world—Russia, India, England, and now Ecuador twice. Through that I've never felt more alive. I believed that God was calling me overseas."

This last trip to Ecuador confirmed it for Jon. Two young missionaries there are leaving next August and Jon fears their efforts will come to a stop. "So," he says, "I'm preparing to go over there in August of 1996. I'll be living in a home for street children— ninety kids from broken homes. I'll be there for spiritual leadership and working as a youth pastor for the two church plants. I'll also be doing pastoral-leadership training for the Quichua Indians who live in the Andes Mountains."

It's a new beginning for Jon. If there's anything that captures his message, it's this: "Whenever people lie on their deathbed, they think about two things: people they love, and God. So I would encourage kids like you who read this book, live for what's most important and don't be deceived by the lies in the world of Satan. Be obedient to God's Word and be a servant to each other."

What about soccer?

He says, for those who want a tip, "Training on your own is the one thing that separates the good players from the great players. Learn ball control, conditioning. If you do that on top of all your practices with your team, you'll excel."

Jon appears headed to make a mark as a missionary and to teach soccer in a place where soccer is loved: Ecuador. Remember to pray for him. He will certainly need all of God's wisdom and strength as he embarks on this new work.

☆ Scott Cook ☆

©1995 by Cindy Skop

Chapter 7

Height: 5 feet, 8 inches

Weight: 155 pounds

Position: Forward

Birth date: October 10, 1964

Team: **Charlotte Eagles**

Scott Cook: Indoor Soccer King

What would you say if you went in to see your family doctor and he took you aside and said, "I want to tell you a message from God!"

Some of us would laugh. Some would be amazed. Most of us probably would think the doctor a little nutty.

But that happened to Scott Cook at a time when he had reached a low point as a Christian, and that message brought him back.

Scott got interested in soccer in grade school at age six. Although his dad wanted him to play football the next year, Scott scored a soccer goal in the last game of the season, and that motivated him to stick with soccer.

Scott's parents were divorced at that time. Though he initially lived with his mother, she became ill, so he went to live with his father in Bethesda, Maryland. When he was ten, his dad signed him up for a local soccer team called the Montgomery United Pintos, coached by two pros from Scotland— John Kerr, Sr., and Gordon Murray. The team had a lot of talent. In fact, Scott had never seen so many good players before, and he ended up not playing that much. But the team won all kinds of tournaments, and Scott stayed with them until his junior year in high school. Incidentally, he and Desmond Armstrong (see story earlier in this book) played against each other that year, Desmond for the Wheaton Boys Club.

Scott went to high school in Rockville, Maryland, and played three years of varsity at center forward, one of the best positions for scoring on the field. His sophomore year he led the team in scoring and tied a school record for most goals in one season—seventeen. *Parade Magazine* made him an all-American during his junior year. Then his senior year he made the *Parade* list and also the High School Coaches list, another widely recognized all-star roster.

Because of his excellence at scoring and offense, Scott was invited to play for the eighteen-and-under national team in a tournament in Acapulco, Mexico. They played against Argentina, Israel, Russia, and other teams. Quite an achievement for a high school senior, but the real highlights were ahead of him.

Scott's first year of college, 1983, he was the star player for Connecticut. The Big East Tournament final that year pitted Connecticut against Syracuse on a cool, sunny afternoon with six thousand people in the stands. Early in the game a Connecticut player made a drive toward the goal and the ball squirted across the top of the penalty area. Scott stood there, ready. It rolled right in front of him. He pulled the trigger, shot, and caught the goalkeeper off guard. It was the first goal in the game. Connecticut went on to win, 5–1.

Connecticut reached the final four in Division I that year, and played their national semifinal game at home. A blizzard roared around them. First it was snow, then freezing rain, then hail. Hazardous conditions. They didn't know which shoes to use. "When you walked on the field," Scott said, "it was like your foot crunched through layers."

They lost the game, 4–0, to Columbia University. Indiana beat Columbia in the final. Scott scored seven goals in the tournament.

That year, Scott was named one of the top sixteen freshmen by *Soccer America Magazine*. Also, he made all-New England and all-Big East. But he had a problem—he was very mixed up. Academics had become a serious problem, and he was not asked to return to school second semester.

The following year he was accepted at the University of South Carolina to play soccer—and to study. In 1985, USC reached the national quarterfinals in Division I and began a tradition of getting to the playoffs every year. Scott made the all-South team his sophomore, junior, and senior years. At one point during Scott's junior year, South Carolina was ranked number one for the first time in its history. Also, he turned himself around academically while at USC.

In that region, a huge rivalry exists between Clemson and South Carolina. Both teams repeatedly vie for number one. Scott says, "We were playing Clemson at home my junior year. They got up on us, 1–0. Then we tied, 1–1. They moved up again, 2–1. Then another tie, 2–2. Then we went ahead, 3–2. They got a penalty kick. Bruce Murray, the son of Gordon Murray, my old coach in Bethesda, Maryland, made the goal. It tied the game. At that point, we went into overtime."

Scott tells how weather conditions affected the players. "Rain damped the field down wet and slimy. Guys on the team were cramping up. Three minutes into overtime (there were two ten-minute halves) I got a throw-in at twenty-five yards out. I shot at twenty yards. It hit the post and went in. We were ahead now, 4–3.

"It was an amazing contest. They tied it up again at 4–4. In the closing minutes of the overtime, my roommate was on the left wing. He shot it across from the far left corner to me at the right post. The cross went over the goalie's outstretched hands. I rushed on to it, dove, and dive-headed it into the goal. So we won, 5–4. There were about three minutes left on the clock."

What a game. But that wasn't the biggie.

In 1986 and 1987, Scott played in the Olympic Festival on the South team, which won the bronze medal the first year and the gold the second. At the 1986 festival Scott scored two goals in four games.

But one wasn't counted.

"I was on the left side of the field in the offensive half. The ball played from the central midfielder over to me, to his left. I came on to it. It was a perfect setup for a one-time shot. I caught everyone off guard, including, apparently, the referees. I cracked it with my right foot. It was in the air, bending in, and it smacked right into the back of the goal, hitting the back netting support. Now, that support was made out of aluminum, but the goalposts were wood. When it hit the aluminum goalpost, it made a ping and bounced out of the goal. Everyone on our team could see it was in. We started celebrating. But the ref had not called it a goal. The other team was still playing and now they were headed off toward our goal. We ran off and stopped them and the ball went out of bounds. The ref didn't call the goal.

"I guess it all worked out, though. We scored later, then they tied. Then I scored the game-winner on a cross that came from the right side and bounced once. On the second bounce I kicked it into the net. We won, 2–1."

Scott was drafted out of college by the Maryland Bays (an outdoor team) of the APSL (American Professional Soccer League), and by two indoor teams: the Baltimore Blast of the MISL (Major Indoor Soccer League) and the Dayton Dynamo of the AISA (American Indoor Soccer Association). He could play for only one indoor league. After training with the Baltimore Blast for two weeks, it looked like he might get cut, so he signed with Dayton.

Scott had an excellent year there. He scored seventeen goals (this was before the three-point system was instituted) and was named to the league's all-rookie team.

For him, as for all the guys in this book, indoor soccer is a different game. Scott says, "It's fast. Like hockey. You have two shifts. One goes in for a minute and a half. The ball careens off the glass and boards. It's much more of an art in outdoor soccer. In indoor it's all fast. You have to possess quickness and speed. I could adapt to it fairly well. Indoor requires your skills to be that much sharper."

Scott's second year at Dayton, the team went 6–14 for the first half of the season. The coach told them at Christmas break to begin to make other plans. In other words, "Look for another job, guys. You ain't stayin' here!"

But the team came back in the new year, went on a massive winning streak, and ended up 20–20, which, in pro soccer, is a very good record. They won their division and their first playoff series, but lost in the championship.

The real highlight, though, came in 1990 while Scott was with the Maryland Bays, a team with great talent. They were preparing to play the San Francisco Blackhawks at Boston University in a game that was to be televised live nationally.

Scott says, "The day before the game we were practicing. I stubbed my toe. I went to see the doctor. He was also the trainer for the team in Orlando, so I knew him a little bit, not well. But I always noticed things were very different about him. He was always kind. Cheerful. Shining.

"While I was there, he complimented our team, saying it was great that we prayed before each game. And then he suddenly said, 'Tomorrow God's going to bless you in a great way.

God told me in a dream last night that you would score two goals tomorrow. The first goal will occur within your first ten minutes in the game. Then you will score another goal.'"

Scott was astonished. He had become something of a lukewarm Christian at that time, but this doctor stunned him into rethinking his position.

He says, "That doctor was very definite. I went back to the clubhouse and told five people about it. Some laughed at me. Two of the guys I told were on the team. One of them laughed at me. The other guy thought it was neat.

"The next day the doctor was taping us up. He had left a small basket of lapel-pin crosses on a table. Different guys on the team put them on their warm-up suits. One I picked up had a backing with a Scripture, Acts 1:8: 'You shall be my witnesses.' So I put the little piece of backing down my right shin guard. I put the cross on my jacket.

"Then we went out to the field. I wasn't a starter. The other team was all over us. It was 0–0 at half-time. San Francisco dominated us something fierce. It looked like a losing contest. Sooner or later, they would score, and keep on scoring. Then, in the second half, the coach put me in. I made a mental note of the time. I wanted to see if this prophecy the doctor had given me would come true.

"The sweeper made a great run up the left side of the field. I was on the right side. He spotted me a great shot in front of the goal. It became a foot race between me and the goalkeeper. I got my foot on it, and it went in. I looked up at the clock. It was just within my first ten minutes. I was amazed.

"I ran over to the bench to find the doctor. I couldn't find him, but the two guys I had told—their eyes were as big as saucers. My one friend held up his index finger for one more goal to go.

"I went back into the game. They scored. 1–1. It went into overtime. No goals. So we went to penalty kicks. I told the coach I wanted to do one. He gave me third place. In a penalty kick like this you have a shootout. Five players on each team take one shot each, alternating: them, us. We shot first. It didn't go in. They shot. Missed. We shot. Made it. They shot. They made it. Tie. Then I was up.

"I did everything wrong mentally. You're supposed to make a decision about which corner you're going for. But all I could think about was that this man had told me I was going to score two goals. So it didn't matter where I shot. So I thought. But at the last second, I kicked hard and straight to a corner. The goalkeeper leaped in the opposite direction. Score! The final score in penalties was 3–2. Since we won the penalty kicks, it counted as one goal. So we finished 2–1.

"At that time in my life I had a lot of doubt and confusion. I had taken some Bible classes at the state-funded school. But it was all very liberal. My life morally was declining. I felt a lot of uncertainty.

"But God reached down and blessed me through this doctor. He had sovereignly ordained this to happen. I was crying because God had shown me I could trust Him. He dispelled all my doubts. I was so excited about it. People came up to interview me after the game. *Soccer International* magazine came by. I told the story. And they printed it. I was His witness, as the little pin had said, and this witness was published internationally. So two prophecies were fulfilled that afternoon! It's the experience I treasure the most in my life."

Scott had become a Christian his sophomore year at USC. After flunking out of the University of Connecticut, he realized he wasn't as good as he thought he was. He really needed stability in his life. Soccer was all-important to him.

"One night a former USC soccer player asked me to go to a rock and roll seminar that taught from a Christian perspective. At the seminar, they challenged me, 'If you know the truth and haven't committed your life to Christ, then you've made a decision against Christ.' They asked us to stand up. I gave my life to the Lord that night."

But it wasn't until 1990 that a doctor with a prophecy turned Scott around forever. Now Scott is attending the Reformed Theological Seminary in Charlotte, planning to go into the ministry.

So what's in the future for a guy who has a heart for the ministry, for missions, for youth, and for soccer? Right now he plays soccer for the Charlotte Eagles and can even see himself as a coach at a Christian college.

There's no question that God is leading Scott Cook. Whether it's in indoor soccer, or outdoor, you can be sure He will be with him to do his best.

Don't miss out on the other books in the Sports Heroes series!

Sports Heroes: Baseball
0-310-49551-2
$4.99

Smashing a winning home run in the ninth inning of a World Series game. Baseball fans dream of it. Joe Carter has done it. Find out what it's like in *Sports Heroes: Baseball*. Plus, meet Orel Hershiser, who pitched 59 consecutive no-run innings—and other great players who share with you the excitement, challenges, and secrets of becoming a major-league star.

Sports Heroes: Basketball
0-310-49561-X
$4.99

Take to the court with some of the NBA's best players. This action-packed book puts you right in the game! Score almost at will with Mark Price's offensive power. Bury opponents with the deadly three-point accuracy of Hersey Hawkins. And find out what some of the greatest stars do *off* the court as well as on it. Here's a thorough look at what it takes to make it in basketball today.

Sports Heroes: Football
0-310-49571-7
$4.99

Go head-to-head with some of the greatest players and coaches in the NFL. *Sports Heroes: Football* will let you taste last-minute victory through Roger Staubach's famous two-minute offense, take you on-field with defensive giant Reggie White, and show you the ins and outs of NFL stardom through the eyes of some of football's biggest stars.

Sports Heroes: Track and Field
0-310-49581-4
$4.99

What would it be like to race world-record-setter Carl Lewis—and win? Leroy Burrell, the runner who beat Lewis to become the fastest man in the world, can tell you. He's just one of the champions you'll meet in *Sports Heroes: Track and Field*—heroes like decathlete Dave Johnson, who won an Olympic medal despite a broken foot. Find out from them what it takes to reach the Olympics in track and field.

Sports Heroes: Soccer
0-310-20264-7
$4.99

Step onto the soccer field with Desmond Armstrong and see what it's like to join the best players on the planet in the World All-Star Game. Meet Brian Davidson, Jon Payne, Scott Cook, and other soccer greats. Discover their best moves . . . and let them show you exactly what it takes to become a professional soccer player today.

Sports Heroes: Summer Olympics
0-310-20266-3
$4.99

Track with Carl Lewis through his stunning career as a four-time Olympian. Find out how Jacqueline Joyner-Kersee overcame a strained tendon to achieve a double-win at the 1988 Olympics. Learn about the victories and setbacks of some of the world's greatest Olympic athletes. They'll inspire you to be the finest athlete you can be!